BLUE & BEAR
The Story Of Stuck Poop

Conceived & Written by Suprita & Dhiraj Gautam
Illustration by Olena Lykova

1

Well, Blue Bear. Ethan doesn't eat many fruits and vegetables or drink enough water every day.

7

8

10

EATING EXPERIMENT

For the next two days, Ethan will eat fruits, green leafy vegetables and drink lots of water.

12

So, reader what do you think happened next?

Why did Blue Bear's tummy hurt and Ethan's did not?

CAN YOU HELP BLUE BEAR IDENTIFY ALL THE VEGETABLES?

(Vegetables are hidden in illustrations)

Finally, heartfelt thank you, for coming along on this ride. We hope you had as much fun as we did. Please take a moment to post a review and tell friends about fun of stuck poop.

Dear Parents & Educators

Thank you for reading Blue Bear and the Story of Stuck Poop with your children. I believe food is an illness, as well as a cure. By choosing foods wisely, we can live a healthy and active life. When children learn healthy eating habits early, they are more likely to retain them.

The Story of Stuck Poop was born from my struggles with weight, healthy eating, and constipation since childhood. As a child I ate whatever I could get my hands on with little regard for my health. I found myself weighing 210 pounds and hypertensive at 28 years of age. In addition to my own health, I witnessed my mother experience many health problems, including heart disease and diabetes. It was then I decided to take control of my life and food choices. By making changes to my food choices and lifestyle I was able to lose 60 pounds. I have maintained my weight loss, and am free from hypertension.

Constipation is a common health problem for children. Blue Bear & The Story of Stuck Poop creates a dialogue for adults to discuss healthy eating, including choosing foods rich in fibers. We can not completely free our world from disease, but we can do our part by making healthy food choices for an active, and healthy life.

Dhiraj Kumar Gautam
Co-Author

Next in the series

BLUE & BEAR

& Hole In The Tooth

Food is Cure

24

Printed in Great Britain
by Amazon

46386323R00016